GARDENING

LOGBOOK

This Book Bloges To

GARDENING LOGBOOK

NAME

LOCATION

SUPPLIER

PRICE

SCIENTIFIC CLASS

VEGETABLE	○	FRUIT
HERB	○	FLOWER
SHRUB	○	TREE
ANNUAL	○	BIENNIAL
PERENNIAL	○	SEEDLING

DATES

GERMINATED

PLANTED

HARVESTED

LIGHT LEVEL

SUN

PARTIAL SUN

SHADE

OTHER

STARTED FROM

SEED

PLANT

RATING

SIZE ○○○○○

COLOR ○○○○○

TASTE ○○○○○

FERTILIZERS & EQUIPMENT

WATER REQUIREMENTS

0%
LESS

CARE INSTRUCTIONS

PLANTING INSTRUCTION

ADDITIONAL NOTES

GARDENING LOGBOOK

NAME

LOCATION

SUPPLIER

PRICE

SCIENTIFIC CLASS

VEGETABLE	○	FRUIT
HERB	○	FLOWER
SHRUB	○	TREE
ANNUAL	○	BIENNIAL
PERENNIAL	○	SEEDLING

DATES

GERMINATED

PLANTED

HARVESTED

LIGHT LEVEL

SUN

PARTIAL SUN

SHADE

OTHER

STARTED FROM

SEED

PLANT

RATING

SIZE ○○○○○

COLOR ○○○○○

TASTE ○○○○○

FERTILIZERS & EQUIPMENT	WATER REQUIREMENTS

0%
LESS

CARE INSTRUCTIONS	PLANTING INSTRUCTION

ADDITIONAL NOTES

GARDENING LOGBOOK

NAME

LOCATION

SUPPLIER

PRICE

SCIENTIFIC CLASS

VEGETABLE ○ FRUIT

HERB ○ FLOWER

SHRUB ○ TREE

ANNUAL ○ BIENNIAL

PERENNIAL ○ SEEDLING

DATES

GERMINATED

PLANTED

HARVESTED

LIGHT LEVEL

SUN

PARTIAL SUN

SHADE

OTHER

STARTED FROM

SEED

PLANT

RATING

SIZE ○○○○○

COLOR ○○○○○

TASTE ○○○○○

FERTILIZERS & EQUIPMENT

WATER REQUIREMENTS

0%
LESS

CARE INSTRUCTIONS

PLANTING INSTRUCTION

ADDITIONAL NOTES

GARDENING LOGBOOK

NAME

LOCATION

SUPPLIER

PRICE

SCIENTIFIC CLASS

VEGETABLE	○		FRUIT
HERB	○		FLOWER
SHRUB	○		TREE
ANNUAL	○		BIENNIAL
PERENNIAL	○		SEEDLING

DATES

GERMINATED

PLANTED

HARVESTED

LIGHT LEVEL

SUN

PARTIAL SUN

SHADE

OTHER

STARTED FROM

SEED

PLANT

RATING

SIZE ○○○○○

COLOR ○○○○○

TASTE ○○○○○

FERTILIZERS & EQUIPMENT

WATER REQUIREMENTS

0%
LESS

CARE INSTRUCTIONS

PLANTING INSTRUCTION

ADDITIONAL NOTES

GARDENING LOGBOOK

NAME

LOCATION

SUPPLIER

PRICE

SCIENTIFIC CLASS

VEGETABLE	○	FRUIT
HERB	○	FLOWER
SHRUB	○	TREE
ANNUAL	○	BIENNIAL
PERENNIAL	○	SEEDLING

DATES

GERMINATED

PLANTED

HARVESTED

LIGHT LEVEL

SUN

PARTIAL SUN

SHADE

OTHER

STARTED FROM

SEED

PLANT

RATING

SIZE ○○○○○

COLOR ○○○○○

TASTE ○○○○○

FERTILIZERS & EQUIPMENT

WATER REQUIREMENTS

0%
LESS

CARE INSTRUCTIONS

PLANTING INSTRUCTION

ADDITIONAL NOTES

GARDENING LOGBOOK

NAME	LOCATION

SUPPLIER	PRICE

SCIENTIFIC CLASS

VEGETABLE	○	FRUIT
HERB	○	FLOWER
SHRUB	○	TREE
ANNUAL	○	BIENNIAL
PERENNIAL	○	SEEDLING

DATES

GERMINATED

PLANTED

HARVESTED

LIGHT LEVEL

SUN

PARTIAL SUN

SHADE

OTHER

STARTED FROM

SEED

PLANT

RATING

SIZE	○○○○○
COLOR	○○○○○
TASTE	○○○○○

FERTILIZERS & EQUIPMENT

WATER REQUIREMENTS

0%
LESS

CARE INSTRUCTIONS

PLANTING INSTRUCTION

ADDITIONAL NOTES

GARDENING LOGBOOK

NAME

LOCATION

SUPPLIER

PRICE

SCIENTIFIC CLASS

VEGETABLE	○	FRUIT
HERB	○	FLOWER
SHRUB	○	TREE
ANNUAL	○	BIENNIAL
PERENNIAL	○	SEEDLING

DATES

GERMINATED

PLANTED

HARVESTED

LIGHT LEVEL

SUN

PARTIAL SUN

SHADE

OTHER

STARTED FROM

SEED

PLANT

RATING

SIZE ○○○○○

COLOR ○○○○○

TASTE ○○○○○

FERTILIZERS & EQUIPMENT

WATER REQUIREMENTS

0%
LESS

CARE INSTRUCTIONS

PLANTING INSTRUCTION

ADDITIONAL NOTES

GARDENING LOGBOOK

NAME		LOCATION	
SUPPLIER		PRICE	

SCIENTIFIC CLASS

VEGETABLE	○	FRUIT	
HERB	○	FLOWER	
SHRUB	○	TREE	
ANNUAL	○	BIENNIAL	
PERENNIAL	○	SEEDLING	

DATES

GERMINATED

PLANTED

HARVESTED

LIGHT LEVEL

SUN

PARTIAL SUN

SHADE

OTHER

STARTED FROM

SEED

PLANT

RATING

SIZE	○○○○○
COLOR	○○○○○
TASTE	○○○○○

FERTILIZERS & EQUIPMENT

WATER REQUIREMENTS

0%
LESS

CARE INSTRUCTIONS

PLANTING INSTRUCTION

ADDITIONAL NOTES

GARDENING LOGBOOK

NAME

LOCATION

SUPPLIER

PRICE

SCIENTIFIC CLASS

VEGETABLE ○ FRUIT

HERB ○ FLOWER

SHRUB ○ TREE

ANNUAL ○ BIENNIAL

PERENNIAL ○ SEEDLING

DATES

GERMINATED

PLANTED

HARVESTED

LIGHT LEVEL

SUN

PARTIAL SUN

SHADE

OTHER

STARTED FROM

SEED

PLANT

RATING

SIZE ○○○○○

COLOR ○○○○○

TASTE ○○○○○

FERTILIZERS & EQUIPMENT

WATER REQUIREMENTS

0%
LESS

CARE INSTRUCTIONS

PLANTING INSTRUCTION

ADDITIONAL NOTES

GARDENING LOGBOOK

NAME

LOCATION

SUPPLIER

PRICE

SCIENTIFIC CLASS

VEGETABLE	○	FRUIT
HERB	○	FLOWER
SHRUB	○	TREE
ANNUAL	○	BIENNIAL
PERENNIAL	○	SEEDLING

DATES

GERMINATED

PLANTED

HARVESTED

LIGHT LEVEL

SUN

PARTIAL SUN

SHADE

OTHER

STARTED FROM

SEED

PLANT

RATING

SIZE ○○○○○

COLOR ○○○○○

TASTE ○○○○○

| **FERTILIZERS & EQUIPMENT** | **WATER REQUIREMENTS** |

0%
LESS

| **CARE INSTRUCTIONS** | **PLANTING INSTRUCTION** |

ADDITIONAL NOTES

GARDENING LOGBOOK

NAME

LOCATION

SUPPLIER

PRICE

SCIENTIFIC CLASS

VEGETABLE	○	FRUIT
HERB	○	FLOWER
SHRUB	○	TREE
ANNUAL	○	BIENNIAL
PERENNIAL	○	SEEDLING

DATES

GERMINATED

PLANTED

HARVESTED

LIGHT LEVEL

SUN

PARTIAL SUN

SHADE

OTHER

STARTED FROM

SEED

PLANT

RATING

SIZE ○○○○○

COLOR ○○○○○

TASTE ○○○○○

FERTILIZERS & EQUIPMENT

WATER REQUIREMENTS

0%
LESS

CARE INSTRUCTIONS

PLANTING INSTRUCTION

ADDITIONAL NOTES

GARDENING LOGBOOK

| NAME | LOCATION |
| SUPPLIER | PRICE |

SCIENTIFIC CLASS

VEGETABLE	○	FRUIT
HERB	○	FLOWER
SHRUB	○	TREE
ANNUAL	○	BIENNIAL
PERENNIAL	○	SEEDLING

DATES

GERMINATED

PLANTED

HARVESTED

LIGHT LEVEL

SUN

PARTIAL SUN

SHADE

OTHER

STARTED FROM

SEED

PLANT

RATING

SIZE	○○○○○
COLOR	○○○○○
TASTE	○○○○○

FERTILIZERS & EQUIPMENT

WATER REQUIREMENTS

0%
LESS

CARE INSTRUCTIONS

PLANTING INSTRUCTION

ADDITIONAL NOTES

GARDENING LOGBOOK

NAME

LOCATION

SUPPLIER

PRICE

SCIENTIFIC CLASS

VEGETABLE	○	FRUIT
HERB	○	FLOWER
SHRUB	○	TREE
ANNUAL	○	BIENNIAL
PERENNIAL	○	SEEDLING

DATES

GERMINATED

PLANTED

HARVESTED

LIGHT LEVEL

SUN

PARTIAL SUN

SHADE

OTHER

STARTED FROM

SEED

PLANT

RATING

SIZE ○○○○○

COLOR ○○○○○

TASTE ○○○○○

FERTILIZERS & EQUIPMENT

WATER REQUIREMENTS

0%
LESS

CARE INSTRUCTIONS

PLANTING INSTRUCTION

ADDITIONAL NOTES

GARDENING LOGBOOK

NAME

LOCATION

SUPPLIER

PRICE

SCIENTIFIC CLASS

VEGETABLE	○	FRUIT
HERB	○	FLOWER
SHRUB	○	TREE
ANNUAL	○	BIENNIAL
PERENNIAL	○	SEEDLING

DATES

GERMINATED

PLANTED

HARVESTED

LIGHT LEVEL

SUN

PARTIAL SUN

SHADE

OTHER

STARTED FROM

SEED

PLANT

RATING

SIZE ○○○○○

COLOR ○○○○○

TASTE ○○○○○

FERTILIZERS & EQUIPMENT

WATER REQUIREMENTS

0%
LESS

CARE INSTRUCTIONS

PLANTING INSTRUCTION

ADDITIONAL NOTES

GARDENING LOGBOOK

NAME

LOCATION

SUPPLIER

PRICE

SCIENTIFIC CLASS

VEGETABLE	○	FRUIT
HERB	○	FLOWER
SHRUB	○	TREE
ANNUAL	○	BIENNIAL
PERENNIAL	○	SEEDLING

DATES

GERMINATED

PLANTED

HARVESTED

LIGHT LEVEL

SUN

PARTIAL SUN

SHADE

OTHER

STARTED FROM

SEED

PLANT

RATING

SIZE ○○○○○

COLOR ○○○○○

TASTE ○○○○○

FERTILIZERS & EQUIPMENT

WATER REQUIREMENTS

0%
LESS

CARE INSTRUCTIONS

PLANTING INSTRUCTION

ADDITIONAL NOTES

GARDENING LOGBOOK

NAME	LOCATION

SUPPLIER	PRICE

SCIENTIFIC CLASS

VEGETABLE	○	FRUIT
HERB	○	FLOWER
SHRUB	○	TREE
ANNUAL	○	BIENNIAL
PERENNIAL	○	SEEDLING

DATES

GERMINATED

PLANTED

HARVESTED

LIGHT LEVEL

SUN

PARTIAL SUN

SHADE

OTHER

STARTED FROM

SEED

PLANT

RATING

SIZE ○○○○○

COLOR ○○○○○

TASTE ○○○○○

FERTILIZERS & EQUIPMENT

WATER REQUIREMENTS

0%
LESS

CARE INSTRUCTIONS

PLANTING INSTRUCTION

ADDITIONAL NOTES

GARDENING LOGBOOK

NAME		LOCATION	
SUPPLIER		PRICE	

SCIENTIFIC CLASS

VEGETABLE	○	FRUIT
HERB	○	FLOWER
SHRUB	○	TREE
ANNUAL	○	BIENNIAL
PERENNIAL	○	SEEDLING

DATES

GERMINATED

PLANTED

HARVESTED

LIGHT LEVEL

SUN

PARTIAL SUN

SHADE

OTHER

STARTED FROM

SEED

PLANT

RATING

SIZE	○○○○○
COLOR	○○○○○
TASTE	○○○○○

FERTILIZERS & EQUIPMENT

WATER REQUIREMENTS

0%
LESS

CARE INSTRUCTIONS

PLANTING INSTRUCTION

ADDITIONAL NOTES

GARDENING LOGBOOK

NAME

LOCATION

SUPPLIER

PRICE

SCIENTIFIC CLASS

VEGETABLE	○	FRUIT
HERB	○	FLOWER
SHRUB	○	TREE
ANNUAL	○	BIENNIAL
PERENNIAL	○	SEEDLING

DATES

GERMINATED

PLANTED

HARVESTED

LIGHT LEVEL

SUN

PARTIAL SUN

SHADE

OTHER

STARTED FROM

SEED

PLANT

RATING

SIZE ○○○○○

COLOR ○○○○○

TASTE ○○○○○

FERTILIZERS & EQUIPMENT

WATER REQUIREMENTS

0%
LESS

CARE INSTRUCTIONS

PLANTING INSTRUCTION

ADDITIONAL NOTES

GARDENING LOGBOOK

NAME

LOCATION

SUPPLIER

PRICE

SCIENTIFIC CLASS

VEGETABLE	○	FRUIT
HERB	○	FLOWER
SHRUB	○	TREE
ANNUAL	○	BIENNIAL
PERENNIAL	○	SEEDLING

DATES

GERMINATED

PLANTED

HARVESTED

LIGHT LEVEL

SUN

PARTIAL SUN

SHADE

OTHER

STARTED FROM

SEED

PLANT

RATING

SIZE ○○○○○

COLOR ○○○○○

TASTE ○○○○○

FERTILIZERS & EQUIPMENT

WATER REQUIREMENTS

0%
LESS

CARE INSTRUCTIONS

PLANTING INSTRUCTION

ADDITIONAL NOTES

GARDENING LOGBOOK

NAME

LOCATION

SUPPLIER

PRICE

SCIENTIFIC CLASS

VEGETABLE	○	FRUIT
HERB	○	FLOWER
SHRUB	○	TREE
ANNUAL	○	BIENNIAL
PERENNIAL	○	SEEDLING

DATES

GERMINATED

PLANTED

HARVESTED

LIGHT LEVEL

SUN

PARTIAL SUN

SHADE

OTHER

STARTED FROM

SEED

PLANT

RATING

SIZE   ○○○○○

COLOR   ○○○○○

TASTE   ○○○○○

FERTILIZERS & EQUIPMENT

WATER REQUIREMENTS

0%
LESS

CARE INSTRUCTIONS

PLANTING INSTRUCTION

ADDITIONAL NOTES

GARDENING LOGBOOK

NAME	LOCATION
SUPPLIER	PRICE

SCIENTIFIC CLASS

VEGETABLE	○	FRUIT
HERB	○	FLOWER
SHRUB	○	TREE
ANNUAL	○	BIENNIAL
PERENNIAL	○	SEEDLING

DATES

GERMINATED

PLANTED

HARVESTED

LIGHT LEVEL

SUN

PARTIAL SUN

SHADE

OTHER

STARTED FROM

SEED

PLANT

RATING

SIZE	○○○○○
COLOR	○○○○○
TASTE	○○○○○

FERTILIZERS & EQUIPMENT

WATER REQUIREMENTS

0%
LESS

CARE INSTRUCTIONS

PLANTING INSTRUCTION

ADDITIONAL NOTES

GARDENING LOGBOOK

NAME

LOCATION

SUPPLIER

PRICE

SCIENTIFIC CLASS

VEGETABLE ○	FRUIT
HERB ○	FLOWER
SHRUB ○	TREE
ANNUAL ○	BIENNIAL
PERENNIAL ○	SEEDLING

DATES

GERMINATED

PLANTED

HARVESTED

LIGHT LEVEL

SUN

PARTIAL SUN

SHADE

OTHER

STARTED FROM

SEED

PLANT

RATING

SIZE ○○○○○

COLOR ○○○○○

TASTE ○○○○○

FERTILIZERS & EQUIPMENT

WATER REQUIREMENTS

0%
LESS

CARE INSTRUCTIONS

PLANTING INSTRUCTION

ADDITIONAL NOTES

GARDENING LOGBOOK

NAME

LOCATION

SUPPLIER

PRICE

SCIENTIFIC CLASS

VEGETABLE	○	FRUIT
HERB	○	FLOWER
SHRUB	○	TREE
ANNUAL	○	BIENNIAL
PERENNIAL	○	SEEDLING

DATES

GERMINATED

PLANTED

HARVESTED

LIGHT LEVEL

SUN

PARTIAL SUN

SHADE

OTHER

STARTED FROM

SEED

PLANT

RATING

SIZE ○○○○○

COLOR ○○○○○

TASTE ○○○○○

FERTILIZERS & EQUIPMENT

WATER REQUIREMENTS

0%
LESS

CARE INSTRUCTIONS

PLANTING INSTRUCTION

ADDITIONAL NOTES

GARDENING LOGBOOK

NAME

LOCATION

SUPPLIER

PRICE

SCIENTIFIC CLASS

VEGETABLE ○ FRUIT

HERB ○ FLOWER

SHRUB ○ TREE

ANNUAL ○ BIENNIAL

PERENNIAL ○ SEEDLING

DATES

GERMINATED

PLANTED

HARVESTED

LIGHT LEVEL

SUN

PARTIAL SUN

SHADE

OTHER

STARTED FROM

SEED

PLANT

RATING

SIZE ○○○○○

COLOR ○○○○○

TASTE ○○○○○

FERTILIZERS & EQUIPMENT

WATER REQUIREMENTS

0%
LESS

CARE INSTRUCTIONS

PLANTING INSTRUCTION

ADDITIONAL NOTES

GARDENING LOGBOOK

| NAME | | LOCATION | |
| SUPPLIER | | PRICE | |

SCIENTIFIC CLASS

VEGETABLE	○	FRUIT
HERB	○	FLOWER
SHRUB	○	TREE
ANNUAL	○	BIENNIAL
PERENNIAL	○	SEEDLING

DATES

GERMINATED

PLANTED

HARVESTED

LIGHT LEVEL

SUN

PARTIAL SUN

SHADE

OTHER

STARTED FROM

SEED

PLANT

RATING

SIZE	○○○○○
COLOR	○○○○○
TASTE	○○○○○

FERTILIZERS & EQUIPMENT

WATER REQUIREMENTS

0%
LESS

CARE INSTRUCTIONS

PLANTING INSTRUCTION

ADDITIONAL NOTES

GARDENING LOGBOOK

NAME		LOCATION
SUPPLIER		PRICE

SCIENTIFIC CLASS

VEGETABLE	○	FRUIT
HERB	○	FLOWER
SHRUB	○	TREE
ANNUAL	○	BIENNIAL
PERENNIAL	○	SEEDLING

DATES

GERMINATED

PLANTED

HARVESTED

LIGHT LEVEL

SUN

PARTIAL SUN

SHADE

OTHER

STARTED FROM

SEED

PLANT

RATING

SIZE	○○○○○
COLOR	○○○○○
TASTE	○○○○○

| FERTILIZERS & EQUIPMENT | WATER REQUIREMENTS |

0%
LESS

| CARE INSTRUCTIONS | PLANTING INSTRUCTION |

ADDITIONAL NOTES

GARDENING LOGBOOK

NAME		LOCATION	
SUPPLIER		PRICE	

SCIENTIFIC CLASS

VEGETABLE	○	FRUIT
HERB	○	FLOWER
SHRUB	○	TREE
ANNUAL	○	BIENNIAL
PERENNIAL	○	SEEDLING

DATES

GERMINATED

PLANTED

HARVESTED

LIGHT LEVEL

SUN

PARTIAL SUN

SHADE

OTHER

STARTED FROM

SEED

PLANT

RATING

SIZE	○○○○○
COLOR	○○○○○
TASTE	○○○○○

FERTILIZERS & EQUIPMENT

WATER REQUIREMENTS

0%
LESS

CARE INSTRUCTIONS

PLANTING INSTRUCTION

ADDITIONAL NOTES

GARDENING LOGBOOK

NAME	LOCATION

SUPPLIER	PRICE

SCIENTIFIC CLASS

VEGETABLE	○	FRUIT
HERB	○	FLOWER
SHRUB	○	TREE
ANNUAL	○	BIENNIAL
PERENNIAL	○	SEEDLING

DATES

GERMINATED

PLANTED

HARVESTED

LIGHT LEVEL

SUN

PARTIAL SUN

SHADE

OTHER

STARTED FROM

SEED

PLANT

RATING

SIZE	○○○○○
COLOR	○○○○○
TASTE	○○○○○

FERTILIZERS & EQUIPMENT

WATER REQUIREMENTS

0%
LESS

CARE INSTRUCTIONS

PLANTING INSTRUCTION

ADDITIONAL NOTES

GARDENING LOGBOOK

NAME	LOCATION
SUPPLIER	PRICE

SCIENTIFIC CLASS

VEGETABLE	○	FRUIT
HERB	○	FLOWER
SHRUB	○	TREE
ANNUAL	○	BIENNIAL
PERENNIAL	○	SEEDLING

DATES

GERMINATED

PLANTED

HARVESTED

LIGHT LEVEL

SUN

PARTIAL SUN

SHADE

OTHER

STARTED FROM

SEED

PLANT

RATING

SIZE	○○○○○
COLOR	○○○○○
TASTE	○○○○○

FERTILIZERS & EQUIPMENT

WATER REQUIREMENTS

0%
LESS

CARE INSTRUCTIONS

PLANTING INSTRUCTION

ADDITIONAL NOTES

GARDENING LOGBOOK

| NAME | | LOCATION | |

| SUPPLIER | | PRICE | |

SCIENTIFIC CLASS

VEGETABLE	○	FRUIT
HERB	○	FLOWER
SHRUB	○	TREE
ANNUAL	○	BIENNIAL
PERENNIAL	○	SEEDLING

DATES

GERMINATED

PLANTED

HARVESTED

LIGHT LEVEL

SUN

PARTIAL SUN

SHADE

OTHER

STARTED FROM

SEED

PLANT

RATING

SIZE ○○○○○

COLOR ○○○○○

TASTE ○○○○○

FERTILIZERS & EQUIPMENT

WATER REQUIREMENTS

0%
LESS

CARE INSTRUCTIONS

PLANTING INSTRUCTION

ADDITIONAL NOTES

GARDENING LOGBOOK

NAME	LOCATION

SUPPLIER	PRICE

SCIENTIFIC CLASS

VEGETABLE	○	FRUIT
HERB	○	FLOWER
SHRUB	○	TREE
ANNUAL	○	BIENNIAL
PERENNIAL	○	SEEDLING

DATES

GERMINATED

PLANTED

HARVESTED

LIGHT LEVEL

SUN

PARTIAL SUN

SHADE

OTHER

STARTED FROM

SEED

PLANT

RATING

SIZE	○○○○○
COLOR	○○○○○
TASTE	○○○○○

FERTILIZERS & EQUIPMENT

WATER REQUIREMENTS

0%
LESS

CARE INSTRUCTIONS

PLANTING INSTRUCTION

ADDITIONAL NOTES

GARDENING LOGBOOK

NAME

LOCATION

SUPPLIER

PRICE

SCIENTIFIC CLASS

VEGETABLE	○	FRUIT
HERB	○	FLOWER
SHRUB	○	TREE
ANNUAL	○	BIENNIAL
PERENNIAL	○	SEEDLING

DATES

GERMINATED

PLANTED

HARVESTED

LIGHT LEVEL

SUN

PARTIAL SUN

SHADE

OTHER

STARTED FROM

SEED

PLANT

RATING

SIZE ○○○○○

COLOR ○○○○○

TASTE ○○○○○

FERTILIZERS & EQUIPMENT

WATER REQUIREMENTS

0%
LESS

CARE INSTRUCTIONS

PLANTING INSTRUCTION

ADDITIONAL NOTES

GARDENING LOGBOOK

NAME		LOCATION	

SUPPLIER		PRICE	

SCIENTIFIC CLASS

VEGETABLE	○	FRUIT
HERB	○	FLOWER
SHRUB	○	TREE
ANNUAL	○	BIENNIAL
PERENNIAL	○	SEEDLING

DATES

GERMINATED

PLANTED

HARVESTED

LIGHT LEVEL

SUN

PARTIAL SUN

SHADE

OTHER

STARTED FROM

SEED

PLANT

RATING

SIZE	○○○○○
COLOR	○○○○○
TASTE	○○○○○

FERTILIZERS & EQUIPMENT

WATER REQUIREMENTS

0%
LESS

CARE INSTRUCTIONS

PLANTING INSTRUCTION

ADDITIONAL NOTES

GARDENING LOGBOOK

NAME		LOCATION
SUPPLIER		PRICE

SCIENTIFIC CLASS

VEGETABLE	◯	FRUIT
HERB	◯	FLOWER
SHRUB	◯	TREE
ANNUAL	◯	BIENNIAL
PERENNIAL	◯	SEEDLING

DATES

GERMINATED

PLANTED

HARVESTED

LIGHT LEVEL

SUN

PARTIAL SUN

SHADE

OTHER

STARTED FROM

SEED

PLANT

RATING

SIZE ◯◯◯◯◯

COLOR ◯◯◯◯◯

TASTE ◯◯◯◯◯

FERTILIZERS & EQUIPMENT

WATER REQUIREMENTS

0%
LESS

CARE INSTRUCTIONS

PLANTING INSTRUCTION

ADDITIONAL NOTES

GARDENING LOGBOOK

NAME	LOCATION

SUPPLIER	PRICE

SCIENTIFIC CLASS

VEGETABLE	○	FRUIT
HERB	○	FLOWER
SHRUB	○	TREE
ANNUAL	○	BIENNIAL
PERENNIAL	○	SEEDLING

DATES

GERMINATED

PLANTED

HARVESTED

LIGHT LEVEL

SUN

PARTIAL SUN

SHADE

OTHER

STARTED FROM

SEED

PLANT

RATING

SIZE	○○○○○
COLOR	○○○○○
TASTE	○○○○○

FERTILIZERS & EQUIPMENT

WATER REQUIREMENTS

0%
LESS

CARE INSTRUCTIONS

PLANTING INSTRUCTION

ADDITIONAL NOTES

GARDENING LOGBOOK

NAME	LOCATION
SUPPLIER	PRICE

SCIENTIFIC CLASS

VEGETABLE	◯	FRUIT
HERB	◯	FLOWER
SHRUB	◯	TREE
ANNUAL	◯	BIENNIAL
PERENNIAL	◯	SEEDLING

DATES

GERMINATED

PLANTED

HARVESTED

LIGHT LEVEL

SUN

PARTIAL SUN

SHADE

OTHER

STARTED FROM

SEED

PLANT

RATING

SIZE	◯◯◯◯◯
COLOR	◯◯◯◯◯
TASTE	◯◯◯◯◯

FERTILIZERS & EQUIPMENT

WATER REQUIREMENTS

0%
LESS

CARE INSTRUCTIONS

PLANTING INSTRUCTION

ADDITIONAL NOTES

GARDENING LOGBOOK

NAME

LOCATION

SUPPLIER

PRICE

SCIENTIFIC CLASS

VEGETABLE	○	FRUIT
HERB	○	FLOWER
SHRUB	○	TREE
ANNUAL	○	BIENNIAL
PERENNIAL	○	SEEDLING

DATES

GERMINATED

PLANTED

HARVESTED

LIGHT LEVEL

SUN

PARTIAL SUN

SHADE

OTHER

STARTED FROM

SEED

PLANT

RATING

SIZE ○○○○○

COLOR ○○○○○

TASTE ○○○○○

FERTILIZERS & EQUIPMENT

WATER REQUIREMENTS

0%
LESS

CARE INSTRUCTIONS

PLANTING INSTRUCTION

ADDITIONAL NOTES

GARDENING LOGBOOK

NAME

LOCATION

SUPPLIER

PRICE

SCIENTIFIC CLASS

VEGETABLE	○	FRUIT
HERB	○	FLOWER
SHRUB	○	TREE
ANNUAL	○	BIENNIAL
PERENNIAL	○	SEEDLING

DATES

GERMINATED

PLANTED

HARVESTED

LIGHT LEVEL

SUN

PARTIAL SUN

SHADE

OTHER

STARTED FROM

SEED

PLANT

RATING

SIZE   ○○○○○

COLOR   ○○○○○

TASTE   ○○○○○

FERTILIZERS & EQUIPMENT

WATER REQUIREMENTS

0%
LESS

CARE INSTRUCTIONS

PLANTING INSTRUCTION

ADDITIONAL NOTES

GARDENING LOGBOOK

NAME		LOCATION	
SUPPLIER		PRICE	

SCIENTIFIC CLASS

VEGETABLE	○	FRUIT
HERB	○	FLOWER
SHRUB	○	TREE
ANNUAL	○	BIENNIAL
PERENNIAL	○	SEEDLING

DATES

GERMINATED

PLANTED

HARVESTED

LIGHT LEVEL

SUN

PARTIAL SUN

SHADE

OTHER

STARTED FROM

SEED

PLANT

RATING

SIZE	○○○○○
COLOR	○○○○○
TASTE	○○○○○

<table>
<tr><td>FERTILIZERS & EQUIPMENT</td><td>WATER REQUIREMENTS</td></tr>
</table>

FERTILIZERS & EQUIPMENT

WATER REQUIREMENTS

0%
LESS

CARE INSTRUCTIONS

PLANTING INSTRUCTION

ADDITIONAL NOTES

GARDENING LOGBOOK

NAME		LOCATION	

SUPPLIER		PRICE	

SCIENTIFIC CLASS

VEGETABLE	○	FRUIT
HERB	○	FLOWER
SHRUB	○	TREE
ANNUAL	○	BIENNIAL
PERENNIAL	○	SEEDLING

DATES

GERMINATED

PLANTED

HARVESTED

LIGHT LEVEL

SUN

PARTIAL SUN

SHADE

OTHER

STARTED FROM

SEED

PLANT

RATING

SIZE	○○○○○
COLOR	○○○○○
TASTE	○○○○○

FERTILIZERS & EQUIPMENT

WATER REQUIREMENTS

0%
LESS

CARE INSTRUCTIONS

PLANTING INSTRUCTION

ADDITIONAL NOTES

GARDENING LOGBOOK

NAME

LOCATION

SUPPLIER

PRICE

SCIENTIFIC CLASS

VEGETABLE	◯	FRUIT	
HERB	◯	FLOWER	
SHRUB	◯	TREE	
ANNUAL	◯	BIENNIAL	
PERENNIAL	◯	SEEDLING	

DATES

GERMINATED

PLANTED

HARVESTED

LIGHT LEVEL

SUN

PARTIAL SUN

SHADE

OTHER

STARTED FROM

SEED

PLANT

RATING

SIZE ◯◯◯◯◯

COLOR ◯◯◯◯◯

TASTE ◯◯◯◯◯

FERTILIZERS & EQUIPMENT

WATER REQUIREMENTS

0%
LESS

CARE INSTRUCTIONS

PLANTING INSTRUCTION

ADDITIONAL NOTES

GARDENING LOGBOOK

NAME	LOCATION

SUPPLIER	PRICE

SCIENTIFIC CLASS

VEGETABLE	○	FRUIT
HERB	○	FLOWER
SHRUB	○	TREE
ANNUAL	○	BIENNIAL
PERENNIAL	○	SEEDLING

DATES

GERMINATED

PLANTED

HARVESTED

LIGHT LEVEL

SUN

PARTIAL SUN

SHADE

OTHER

STARTED FROM

SEED

PLANT

RATING

SIZE ○○○○○

COLOR ○○○○○

TASTE ○○○○○

FERTILIZERS & EQUIPMENT

WATER REQUIREMENTS

0%
LESS

CARE INSTRUCTIONS

PLANTING INSTRUCTION

ADDITIONAL NOTES

GARDENING LOGBOOK

NAME

LOCATION

SUPPLIER

PRICE

SCIENTIFIC CLASS

VEGETABLE ○ FRUIT

HERB ○ FLOWER

SHRUB ○ TREE

ANNUAL ○ BIENNIAL

PERENNIAL ○ SEEDLING

DATES

GERMINATED

PLANTED

HARVESTED

LIGHT LEVEL

SUN

PARTIAL SUN

SHADE

OTHER

STARTED FROM

SEED

PLANT

RATING

SIZE ○○○○

COLOR ○○○○

TASTE ○○○○

FERTILIZERS & EQUIPMENT

WATER REQUIREMENTS

0%
LESS

CARE INSTRUCTIONS

PLANTING INSTRUCTION

ADDITIONAL NOTES

GARDENING LOGBOOK

NAME

LOCATION

SUPPLIER

PRICE

SCIENTIFIC CLASS

VEGETABLE	○	FRUIT
HERB	○	FLOWER
SHRUB	○	TREE
ANNUAL	○	BIENNIAL
PERENNIAL	○	SEEDLING

DATES

GERMINATED

PLANTED

HARVESTED

LIGHT LEVEL

SUN

PARTIAL SUN

SHADE

OTHER

STARTED FROM

SEED

PLANT

RATING

SIZE ○○○○○

COLOR ○○○○○

TASTE ○○○○○

FERTILIZERS & EQUIPMENT

WATER REQUIREMENTS

0%
LESS

CARE INSTRUCTIONS

PLANTING INSTRUCTION

ADDITIONAL NOTES

GARDENING LOGBOOK

NAME		LOCATION
SUPPLIER		PRICE

SCIENTIFIC CLASS

VEGETABLE	○	FRUIT
HERB	○	FLOWER
SHRUB	○	TREE
ANNUAL	○	BIENNIAL
PERENNIAL	○	SEEDLING

DATES

GERMINATED

PLANTED

HARVESTED

LIGHT LEVEL

SUN

PARTIAL SUN

SHADE

OTHER

STARTED FROM

SEED

PLANT

RATING

SIZE	○○○○○
COLOR	○○○○○
TASTE	○○○○○

FERTILIZERS & EQUIPMENT

WATER REQUIREMENTS

0%
LESS

CARE INSTRUCTIONS

PLANTING INSTRUCTION

ADDITIONAL NOTES

GARDENING LOGBOOK

NAME	LOCATION

SUPPLIER	PRICE

SCIENTIFIC CLASS

VEGETABLE	○	FRUIT
HERB	○	FLOWER
SHRUB	○	TREE
ANNUAL	○	BIENNIAL
PERENNIAL	○	SEEDLING

DATES

GERMINATED

PLANTED

HARVESTED

LIGHT LEVEL

SUN

PARTIAL SUN

SHADE

OTHER

STARTED FROM

SEED

PLANT

RATING

SIZE	○○○○○
COLOR	○○○○○
TASTE	○○○○○

FERTILIZERS & EQUIPMENT

WATER REQUIREMENTS

0%
LESS

CARE INSTRUCTIONS

PLANTING INSTRUCTION

ADDITIONAL NOTES

GARDENING LOGBOOK

NAME	LOCATION

SUPPLIER	PRICE

SCIENTIFIC CLASS

VEGETABLE	○	FRUIT
HERB	○	FLOWER
SHRUB	○	TREE
ANNUAL	○	BIENNIAL
PERENNIAL	○	SEEDLING

DATES

GERMINATED

PLANTED

HARVESTED

LIGHT LEVEL

SUN

PARTIAL SUN

SHADE

OTHER

STARTED FROM

SEED

PLANT

RATING

SIZE	○○○○○
COLOR	○○○○○
TASTE	○○○○○

FERTILIZERS & EQUIPMENT

WATER REQUIREMENTS

0%
LESS

CARE INSTRUCTIONS

PLANTING INSTRUCTION

ADDITIONAL NOTES

GARDENING LOGBOOK

NAME		LOCATION
SUPPLIER		PRICE

SCIENTIFIC CLASS

VEGETABLE	○	FRUIT
HERB	○	FLOWER
SHRUB	○	TREE
ANNUAL	○	BIENNIAL
PERENNIAL	○	SEEDLING

DATES

GERMINATED

PLANTED

HARVESTED

LIGHT LEVEL

SUN

PARTIAL SUN

SHADE

OTHER

STARTED FROM

SEED

PLANT

RATING

SIZE ○○○○○

COLOR ○○○○○

TASTE ○○○○○

FERTILIZERS & EQUIPMENT

WATER REQUIREMENTS

0%
LESS

CARE INSTRUCTIONS

PLANTING INSTRUCTION

ADDITIONAL NOTES

GARDENING LOGBOOK

NAME

LOCATION

SUPPLIER

PRICE

SCIENTIFIC CLASS

VEGETABLE ○		FRUIT
HERB ○		FLOWER
SHRUB ○		TREE
ANNUAL ○		BIENNIAL
PERENNIAL ○		SEEDLING

DATES

GERMINATED

PLANTED

HARVESTED

LIGHT LEVEL

SUN

PARTIAL SUN

SHADE

OTHER

STARTED FROM

SEED

PLANT

RATING

SIZE ○○○○○

COLOR ○○○○○

TASTE ○○○○○

FERTILIZERS & EQUIPMENT

WATER REQUIREMENTS

0%
LESS

CARE INSTRUCTIONS

PLANTING INSTRUCTION

ADDITIONAL NOTES

GARDENING LOGBOOK

NAME	LOCATION

SUPPLIER	PRICE

SCIENTIFIC CLASS

VEGETABLE	○	FRUIT
HERB	○	FLOWER
SHRUB	○	TREE
ANNUAL	○	BIENNIAL
PERENNIAL	○	SEEDLING

DATES

GERMINATED

PLANTED

HARVESTED

LIGHT LEVEL

SUN

PARTIAL SUN

SHADE

OTHER

STARTED FROM

SEED

PLANT

RATING

SIZE	○○○○○
COLOR	○○○○○
TASTE	○○○○○

FERTILIZERS & EQUIPMENT

WATER REQUIREMENTS

0%
LESS

CARE INSTRUCTIONS

PLANTING INSTRUCTION

ADDITIONAL NOTES

GARDENING LOGBOOK

NAME

LOCATION

SUPPLIER

PRICE

SCIENTIFIC CLASS

VEGETABLE	○	FRUIT
HERB	○	FLOWER
SHRUB	○	TREE
ANNUAL	○	BIENNIAL
PERENNIAL	○	SEEDLING

DATES

GERMINATED

PLANTED

HARVESTED

LIGHT LEVEL

SUN

PARTIAL SUN

SHADE

OTHER

STARTED FROM

SEED

PLANT

RATING

SIZE ○○○○○

COLOR ○○○○○

TASTE ○○○○○

FERTILIZERS & EQUIPMENT

WATER REQUIREMENTS

0%
LESS

CARE INSTRUCTIONS

PLANTING INSTRUCTION

ADDITIONAL NOTES

GARDENING LOGBOOK

NAME

LOCATION

SUPPLIER

PRICE

SCIENTIFIC CLASS

VEGETABLE	○	FRUIT
HERB	○	FLOWER
SHRUB	○	TREE
ANNUAL	○	BIENNIAL
PERENNIAL	○	SEEDLING

DATES

GERMINATED

PLANTED

HARVESTED

LIGHT LEVEL

SUN

PARTIAL SUN

SHADE

OTHER

STARTED FROM

SEED

PLANT

RATING

SIZE ○○○○○

COLOR ○○○○○

TASTE ○○○○○

FERTILIZERS & EQUIPMENT

WATER REQUIREMENTS

0%
LESS

CARE INSTRUCTIONS

PLANTING INSTRUCTION

ADDITIONAL NOTES

GARDENING LOGBOOK

NAME	LOCATION

SUPPLIER	PRICE

SCIENTIFIC CLASS

VEGETABLE	○	FRUIT
HERB	○	FLOWER
SHRUB	○	TREE
ANNUAL	○	BIENNIAL
PERENNIAL	○	SEEDLING

DATES

GERMINATED

PLANTED

HARVESTED

LIGHT LEVEL

SUN

PARTIAL SUN

SHADE

OTHER

STARTED FROM

SEED

PLANT

RATING

SIZE	○○○○○
COLOR	○○○○○
TASTE	○○○○○

FERTILIZERS & EQUIPMENT

WATER REQUIREMENTS

0%
LESS

CARE INSTRUCTIONS

PLANTING INSTRUCTION

ADDITIONAL NOTES

GARDENING LOGBOOK

NAME

LOCATION

SUPPLIER

PRICE

SCIENTIFIC CLASS

VEGETABLE	○	FRUIT
HERB	○	FLOWER
SHRUB	○	TREE
ANNUAL	○	BIENNIAL
PERENNIAL	○	SEEDLING

DATES

GERMINATED

PLANTED

HARVESTED

LIGHT LEVEL

SUN

PARTIAL SUN

SHADE

OTHER

STARTED FROM

SEED

PLANT

RATING

SIZE ○○○○○

COLOR ○○○○○

TASTE ○○○○○

FERTILIZERS & EQUIPMENT

WATER REQUIREMENTS

0%
LESS

CARE INSTRUCTIONS

PLANTING INSTRUCTION

ADDITIONAL NOTES

GARDENING LOGBOOK

NAME

LOCATION

SUPPLIER

PRICE

SCIENTIFIC CLASS

VEGETABLE	○	FRUIT
HERB	○	FLOWER
SHRUB	○	TREE
ANNUAL	○	BIENNIAL
PERENNIAL	○	SEEDLING

DATES

GERMINATED

PLANTED

HARVESTED

LIGHT LEVEL

SUN

PARTIAL SUN

SHADE

OTHER

STARTED FROM

SEED

PLANT

RATING

SIZE ○○○○○

COLOR ○○○○○

TASTE ○○○○○

FERTILIZERS & EQUIPMENT

WATER REQUIREMENTS

0%
LESS

CARE INSTRUCTIONS

PLANTING INSTRUCTION

ADDITIONAL NOTES

GARDENING LOGBOOK

NAME

LOCATION

SUPPLIER

PRICE

SCIENTIFIC CLASS

VEGETABLE	○	FRUIT
HERB	○	FLOWER
SHRUB	○	TREE
ANNUAL	○	BIENNIAL
PERENNIAL	○	SEEDLING

DATES

GERMINATED

PLANTED

HARVESTED

LIGHT LEVEL

SUN

PARTIAL SUN

SHADE

OTHER

STARTED FROM

SEED

PLANT

RATING

SIZE ○○○○○

COLOR ○○○○○

TASTE ○○○○○

FERTILIZERS & EQUIPMENT

WATER REQUIREMENTS

0%
LESS

CARE INSTRUCTIONS

PLANTING INSTRUCTION

ADDITIONAL NOTES

GARDENING LOGBOOK

NAME

LOCATION

SUPPLIER

PRICE

SCIENTIFIC CLASS

VEGETABLE	○	FRUIT
HERB	○	FLOWER
SHRUB	○	TREE
ANNUAL	○	BIENNIAL
PERENNIAL	○	SEEDLING

DATES

GERMINATED

PLANTED

HARVESTED

LIGHT LEVEL

SUN

PARTIAL SUN

SHADE

OTHER

STARTED FROM

SEED

PLANT

RATING

SIZE ○○○○○

COLOR ○○○○○

TASTE ○○○○○

FERTILIZERS & EQUIPMENT

WATER REQUIREMENTS

0%
LESS

CARE INSTRUCTIONS

PLANTING INSTRUCTION

ADDITIONAL NOTES

GARDENING LOGBOOK

NAME

LOCATION

SUPPLIER

PRICE

SCIENTIFIC CLASS

VEGETABLE ○		FRUIT
HERB ○		FLOWER
SHRUB ○		TREE
ANNUAL ○		BIENNIAL
PERENNIAL ○		SEEDLING

DATES

GERMINATED

PLANTED

HARVESTED

LIGHT LEVEL

SUN

PARTIAL SUN

SHADE

OTHER

STARTED FROM

SEED

PLANT

RATING

SIZE ○○○○○

COLOR ○○○○○

TASTE ○○○○○

FERTILIZERS & EQUIPMENT

WATER REQUIREMENTS

0%
LESS

CARE INSTRUCTIONS

PLANTING INSTRUCTION

ADDITIONAL NOTES

GARDENING LOGBOOK

NAME

LOCATION

SUPPLIER

PRICE

SCIENTIFIC CLASS

VEGETABLE	○	FRUIT
HERB	○	FLOWER
SHRUB	○	TREE
ANNUAL	○	BIENNIAL
PERENNIAL	○	SEEDLING

DATES

GERMINATED

PLANTED

HARVESTED

LIGHT LEVEL

SUN

PARTIAL SUN

SHADE

OTHER

STARTED FROM

SEED

PLANT

RATING

SIZE ○○○○○

COLOR ○○○○○

TASTE ○○○○○

FERTILIZERS & EQUIPMENT

WATER REQUIREMENTS

0%
LESS

CARE INSTRUCTIONS

PLANTING INSTRUCTION

ADDITIONAL NOTES

GARDENING LOGBOOK

NAME

LOCATION

SUPPLIER

PRICE

SCIENTIFIC CLASS

VEGETABLE	○	FRUIT
HERB	○	FLOWER
SHRUB	○	TREE
ANNUAL	○	BIENNIAL
PERENNIAL	○	SEEDLING

DATES

GERMINATED

PLANTED

HARVESTED

LIGHT LEVEL

SUN

PARTIAL SUN

SHADE

OTHER

STARTED FROM

SEED

PLANT

RATING

SIZE ○○○○○

COLOR ○○○○○

TASTE ○○○○○

FERTILIZERS & EQUIPMENT

WATER REQUIREMENTS

0%
LESS

CARE INSTRUCTIONS

PLANTING INSTRUCTION

ADDITIONAL NOTES